P9-DDI-129

DISCARD

WEST GEORGIA REGIONAL LIBRARY SYSTEM
Neva Lomason Memorial Library

Living Fossils

LIVING FOSSILS

By Cass R. Sandak

Franklin Watts
New York / London / Toronto / Sydney
A First Book

Acknowledgments

The author would like to thank Dr. Carl George of the Biology Department of Union College, Schenectady, New York, and Jin Meng of the American Museum of Natural History in New York City for their many valuable suggestions.

Cover photography copyright ©: Animals Animals/W. Gregory Brown

Photographs copyright ©: Comstock Photography, N.Y.: pp. 2, 10 (both Franklin J. Viola), 8 top (Jack K. Clark), 8 center, 30 bottom (both Russ Kinne), 8 bottom (Phyllis Greenberg), 13 (Michael S. Thompson); Breck P. Kent: pp. 17, 23 bottom, 24 bottom, 51 right; Animals Animals/Earth Scenes: pp. 20 top (OSF), 24 top (Jack Wilburn), 28 (L.L.T. Rhodes), 30 top (Zig Leszczynski), 33 (Richard K. LaVal), 39, 41 bottom (both Doug Wechsler), 45 top (Fritz Prenzel), 45 bottom (Kathie Atkinson/OSF), 47 (Mickey Gibson), 53 top (Fred Whitehead), 53 bottom (Michael Fogden); Visuals Unlimited: pp. 23 top (Daniel Gotshall), 20 bottom (William Jorgensen); Jeff Foott Productions: pp. 41 top, 51 left.

Library of Congress Cataloging-in-Publication Data

Sandak, Cass R.
    Living fossils / by Cass R. Sandak.
      p.   cm. — (A First book)
    Includes bibliographical references and index.
    Summary: Describes plants and animals that developed in ancient times and remain relatively unchanged today, including the cockroach, opossum, and ginkgo tree.
    ISBN 0-531-20048-5
    1. Living fossils—Juvenile literature. [1. Living fossils.]
I. Title. II. Series.
QL88.5.S26   1992
574—dc20   91-34423 CIP AC

COPYRIGHT © 1992 BY CASS R. SANDAK
ALL RIGHTS RESERVED
PRINTED IN THE UNITED STATES OF AMERICA
6 5 4 3 2 1

Contents

How Can a Fossil Be Living?

You don't need to look far to find a living **fossil**. A **ginkgo** tree with its fan-shaped leaves may be growing in a nearby park or garden. A dragonfly may buzz through an open window, or a silverfish, a cockroach, or even a scorpion may scurry through a room in your house. An opossum may inhabit your backyard. All of these are "living fossils." They are living links with the remote past.

Fossils are the parts or remains of a plant or an animal that have been turned to stone or left an imprint or hollow in the stone. On rare occasions, fossil remains have been preserved in hardened resin or amber, or some other medium such as peat. Certain fossils are

called "trace fossils." They are evidence of ancient life-forms such as tracks or footprints hardened into stone.

By definition, fossils are the remains of dead things. How then can we talk about "living" fossils? Living fossils are examples of currently living organisms that developed in very ancient times and have remained relatively unchanged. Living fossils have usually survived longer than the other forms of life they developed with. The process of **evolution** has changed the basic form and behavior of almost all plants and animals. But the **species** of plants and animals that we call living fossils have remained largely untouched by these changes.

Some living fossils are common, well-known species—cockroaches and opossums fit into this category. They have a broad adaptability that has allowed them to survive. They are cases of "arrested" evolution—types of organisms that have simply stopped changing. Other living fossils are somewhat rare survivors, such as the ginkgo tree or the horseshoe crab. And some living fossils are older than others.

The cockroach (top), scorpion (center), and opossum (bottom) are all closely related to prehistoric animal species.

9

The earth was formed about 4.5 billion years ago. According to scientists' estimates, life originated in the seas about 3 billion years ago. Few fossils are found in rocks older than 600 million years. Some living things existed before then, but these earliest life-forms were mostly simple one-celled organisms. They were small and had mostly body parts that did not readily become fossilized. Still scientists believe these simplest life-forms have not changed much since they first appeared.

Paleontologists are scientists who study fossils to try to piece together the story of life on earth. They study plant and animal fossils, just as botanists and zoologists study living plants and animals.

The fossil record has many gaps. A lot of scientific guesswork goes into reconstructing earth's natural history. There are organisms living today that have remained unchanged for half a billion years or more. Other living fossils date back only 100 million years or less.

The horseshoe crab found along the eastern coast of the United States is a relative of the ancient trilobites.

Chapter One

The Tree of Life

Darwin and Evolution

The nineteenth-century British naturalist Charles Darwin coined the phrase "living fossil." He wrote of them: "They have endured to the present day from having inhabited a confined area, and from having been exposed to less varied, and therefore less severe, competition." Darwin thought of living fossils as organisms that evolved at very slow rates. Many millions of years and thousands of generations are needed for new life-forms to develop.

Darwin used the term "living fossil" in talking about one species, the Chinese tree *Ginkgo biloba*. Certainly there are some extremely rare and exotic plants and animals that seem to fit Darwin's definition. But some living fossils are not rare at all.

Darwin was twenty-two when he was invited to sail as the official naturalist on the voyage of the *Beagle*. This was a scientific expedition sponsored by the British

The ginkgo tree is a living remnant of the Age of Dinosaurs.

government. In the course of the five-year-long journey he compiled information on animal diversity around the world. This he used as evidence for his theory of evolution based on the process of natural selection.

After he returned to England, Darwin continued his research and writings and mulled over his theories. He was fifty years old in 1859 when his book *On the Origin of the Species* was published. Darwin believed that evolution creates new species through the process of natural selection.

The Driving Forces of Evolution

Many more individuals are born than can survive to reproduce and live to old age. There is, therefore, a competition for survival that allows the fittest to survive. The meaning of "fittest" varies. In some cases it means the strongest or fastest. But in other cases it may be the smallest and most elusive. The individuals most fit for survival live to maturity. They reproduce and pass on those traits that helped them to survive. This process is called **"natural selection"** and is the core of Darwin's theory.

Evolution gives rise to new species of animals and plants through **mutation** and **adaptation,** as well as natural selection. Every time living things reproduce, **genetic** material is copied. Most often it is reshuffled and recombined. This is why offspring that have the same parents and the same ancestry show individuality.

14

T I M E   S C A L E

Era	Periods (Epochs or Ages)	Millions of Years Ago (Duration in Parentheses)	Evolutionary Developments (From latest to earliest)
Present			
CENOZOIC	Quaternary		
	Holocene		
	Pleistocene	1	modern man develops
	Upper Tertiary		
	Pliocene	13 (12)	mankind's ancestors continue to develop
	Miocene	25 (2)	development of bulk of modern species; mankind's earliest ancestors develop
	Lower Tertiary		more advanced mammalian forms
	Oligocene	36 (`1)	
	Eocene	58 (22)	hoofed animals and carnivores develop;
	Paleocene	63 (5)	explosive increases in mammal diversity; palms and broad-leaved angiosperms flourish
MESOZOIC	Cretaceous	135 (72)	close of Cretaceous—extinction of dinosaurs and many other life-forms; opossums and insectivores develop; mammals are still small and insignificant; monotreme and marsupial mammals develop; magnolia, maple, oak and many other trees develop, expansion of mammals and birds; first flowering plants (angiosperms)
	Jurassic	180 (45)	many modern insects; ginkgos widespread, but soon become all but extinct; earliest mammals (primitive and rodent-like); oldest birds develop; dinosaurs dominate; flying reptiles develop
	Triassic	230 (50)	primitive conifers and cycads flourish; lobster-like arthropods develop; new types of sponges and protozoans; earliest dinosaurs; reptiles establish dominance on sea and land
PALEOZOIC	Permian	280 (50)	extinction of trilobites; extinction of certain corals, most crinoids and cephalopods; many insects: beetles and true dragonflies; earliest reptiles— similar to amphibians; variety of fishes; early conifers replace primitive coal forests
	Pennsylvanian (Upper Carboniferous)	310 (30)	great coal-swamp forests, including huge scale trees (lycopods), seed ferns and giant horsetails; many amphibians; giant dragonflies
	Mississippian (Lower Carboniferous)	345 (35)	warm shallow seas; amphibians diversify; corals, brachiopods and crinoids flourish

continued on next page

Era	Periods (Epochs or Ages)	Millions of Years Ago (Duration in Parentheses)	Evolutionary Developments (From latest to earliest)
	Devonian	405 (60)	Late Devonian—forest of scale trees and seed ferns; oldest spiders, millipedes and insects—silverfish develop; trilobites diminishing; expansion of fishes and land plants; first land animals—the earliest amphibians; jawless fishes, cartilaginous fishes, early bony fishes, crossopterygians/lobe-finned fishes
	Silurian	425 (20)	greater diversification of plants and animals; earliest land plants appear; giant marine scorpion-like creatures; shallow seas—primitive fishes
	Ordovician	500 (75)	Late Ordovician—first land plants; first vertebrates—ostracaderm fishes; giant cephalopods; crinoids appear
	Cambrian	600 (100)	arthropods develop; brachiopods and echinoderms develop; trilobites develop; first common widespread fossils
Pre-Cambrian PROTEROZOIC	not divided into periods	1.4 billion (800)	fossils are rare; algae, fungi, jellyfish, worm casts and tracks
ARCHEOZOIC		2.3 billion (900) 4.6 billion years ago: earth formed	algae and radiolarian remains (oldest exceed 2 billion years)

Mutations are changes in genetic material that introduce **variations** in the form of plants or animals. The traits produced by genetic mutation may give some individuals a survival advantage. This adaptation to the environment may be passed on from generation to generation.

Isolated breeding populations have their own sets of genetic **traits**, known as **gene pools.** This leads to new varieties of plants and animals that may become new species. If plants and animals fail to adapt or evolve fast enough, they can become extinct.

Ammonite fossils of the Jurassic period, from the Bavarian region of Germany. Ammonites, now extinct, were a type of mollusk.

Certain adaptations make some species well suited for their environment. They are good candidates to become living fossils. These creatures are so adaptable they can adjust easily to almost any changes in the environment. Such organisms seem to have stopped evolving. They have reached a point of adaptation that makes further changes unnecessary.

Reasons for slow evolution include low rates of mutation and of genetic variability. Environments that are stable for long periods tend to weed out fewer "unfit" individuals. An organism that is already well adapted to an environment has no reason to evolve or change.

Some living fossils are more conservative than other species. They hold on to ancient characteristics. They also resist change and do not show a wide range of diversity. These animals are able to stand up to changes that have occurred in earth's environment in the long periods since these species first appeared.

Many living fossils seem to have certain features in common. Often they have comparatively long life spans as individuals. This tends to slow down evolution, since the fewer the generations, the fewer the opportunities for genetic changes. Many or most living fossils are very adaptable. They show a surprising ability to adjust to life's conditions. Animals that are not too "fussy" or too narrow in their needs have a better chance of surviving.

Chapter Two

The Life of the Sea

Life arose in the seas probably some 3 billion years ago. The earliest and simplest forms of invertebrates (animals without backbones) developed in the sea and some of the same forms still survive there. By far, the most ancient examples of living fossils are the **radiolarians** (ray-dee-o-LAR-ee-ans). Radiolarians are various types of microscopic, or very small, one-celled animals. Some have remained basically the same in body shape for well over 2 billion years.

Marine environments are generally stable. Water temperatures do not vary much. Nutrients are plentiful. Sea predators may be a threat, so often it is the small, seemingly insignificant and out-of-the-way types of animals that have survived to become living fossils.

(Above) Radiolarians are
microscopic, one-celled
animals. The structure of
many types of radiolarians
has remained unchanged
since the Cambrian period.
(Left) *Neopilina*, the
"worm snail," an exotic
creature first discovered
off the western coast
of Mexico in 1952.

One such oddity is the **neopilina** (NEE-o-pil-ee-na). This "worm snail" was discovered in 1952 by a Danish expedition on the ship *Galathea*. The ocean-dwelling mollusk *Neopilina galathae* is about the size of a silver dollar. Before 1952, scientists had believed that neopilina had been extinct for more than 350 million years. It was first caught in 2-mile-deep (3 km) water off the western coast of Mexico. This organism is a link between hard-shelled mollusks and soft-bodied, segmented worms such as earthworms. The neopilina has more than a 500-million-year history and before 1952 was known only from fossil specimens.

Trilobites were a dominant form of animal life more than 300 million years ago, but now the entire class of animals is extinct. In its early stage of development the immature **horseshoe crab** (genus *Limulus*—pronounced LIM-yoo-lus) closely resembles the trilobite and is its closest living relative. The horseshoe crab survives in only two parts of the globe—on the U.S. Atlantic coast and on the islands of Indonesia, half a world away. The squat, flat animal has a bell-shaped "head," or prosoma, made from several fused segments. It has six pairs of legs and is not really a crab at all, but a relative of the spider. The present-day horseshoe crab is the same in structure as its remote ancestors.

The **lingula** (LING-yoo-la) is a brachiopod, a small marine invertebrate with a soft body enclosed in a shell with two unequal tongue-shaped valves. It is nearly identical to fossil specimens that date back 600 million years. The lingula burrows in the sand in warm, shallow coastal waters in many parts of the world. The creature first appeared in the early Cambrian period—at the beginning of the Paleozoic era. It is tough and adaptable and can live for long periods in partly fresh water. It can survive hours of exposure to the air when left on tidal flats. The lingula also flourishes in environments where pollution has killed off other marine animals.

The **sea lily** is not really a plant at all, but an animal related to starfish, sand dollars, and sea urchins. The sea lily is a "crinoid" (CRY-noyd). It is related to ancient animals (also called crinoids), with colorful, flowerlike crowns of fine, waving "petals" that catch small animals swimming nearby. Specimens of crinoid fossils can be several feet long, although the fossils are brittle and are usually found broken into small segments. Most modern sea lily specimens are only about 4 inches (10 cm) tall.

Sea lilies first appeared more than 500 million years ago during the Ordovician period. In the Mississippian age (370 million years ago), most of North America was covered by a shallow sea filled with hun-

(Right) A sea lily, a modern crinoid. (Below) A fossil specimen of an ancient crinoid, *Barycrinus princeps,* dating from the Mississippian period. The fossil was found in Crawfordsville, Indiana.

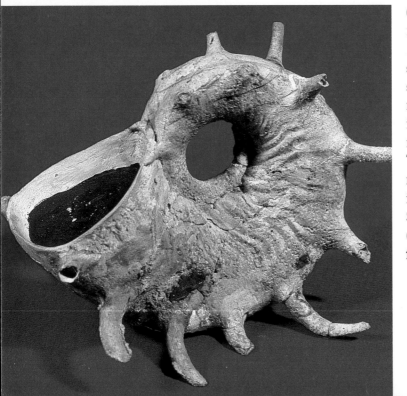

(Above) A chambered
nautilus, *Nautilus compilus.*
It is a member of the sole
surviving genus of a
subclass known as the
nautiloids that flourished
in the seas some 200
million years ago.
Today the chambered
nautilus is found
in the Indian and
South Pacific oceans.
(Below) A nautiloid
fossil found in Texas.

dreds of species of sea lily. Today in the Mississippi valley the remains of this undersea "garden" of crinoids form a mass of fossil-bearing limestone 200 to 500 feet (70 to 150 m) thick that covers many thousands of square miles. Until 1836, sea lilies were known only from fossil evidence. In that year, a dredge pulled up some samples of living sea lilies from the ocean depths, and other species have been discovered since then.

The **nautilus** (NAW-til-us), or chambered nautilus, is one of the most intriguing and graceful of the living fossils. It is the sole surviving **genus** (there are several species) of a subclass called the nautiloids. The nautiloids flourished in the sea more than 200 million years ago. Today's species of nautilus are confined to the deep waters of the Indian and South Pacific oceans.

The nautilus has a spirally coiled shell made up of a series of hollow chambers. As the nautilus grows, it secretes a succession of larger chambers. The soft body of the animal is housed in the newest and largest of the chambers it has formed. A tubelike extension, the "siphuncle," stretches through the nautilus's body. The animal breathes by means of gills that filter gases out of the seawater. It pumps air through the siphuncle into the older, empty chambers of the spiral. These air-filled chambers give the animal enough buoyancy to allow it to swim.

Chapter Three

The World of Fishes

The Age of Fishes

Fishes were the first vertebrates—animals with back-bones. They became common during the Devonian period, the Age of Fishes, approximately 400 million years ago.

The earliest fishes were jawless. The only types of jawless fish living today are the hagfish and the lamprey—both living fossils. Among the several early groups of fishes, the *crossopterygians* (cross-op-ter-IJ-yams), the "fringe-finned" or "lobe-finned" fishes, are best known from fossils. Their fins strongly resembled flippers. Some of these fish walked on their fleshy fins and crawled out of the sea.

The Coelacanth:
The Star of Living Fossils

The **coelacanth** (SEE-la-kanth) is the only known living representation of the crossopterygians. It is probably the most famous living fossil. We know that the fish evolved more than 400 million years ago. In 1839 the Swiss naturalist Louis Agassiz examined the first coelacanth fossil. It was a 250-million-year-old specimen found during the construction of an English railroad. Scientists believed that the fish had been extinct for 70 million years. That was until 1939, when a *living* coelacanth was discovered in the Indian Ocean near Madagascar. According to scientists, most features of the coelacanth had been established by the late Devonian period.

The coelacanth is an important link between marine and land vertebrates. The name, from the Greek, means "hollow spine" and refers to the small spines that support the fins. During the Devonian period, fish similar to the coelacanth walked out of the sea. They changed from sea to land dwellers. Descendants of these fish gave rise to **amphibians.** The amphibians, in turn, became the ancestors of the reptiles, birds, and mammals.

The coelacanth might still be unknown today were it not for the quick thinking of Margaret Courtney-

Latimer, the curator of a South African science museum. When the unusual specimen was brought to her, she didn't recognize what it was. But she did know that it was both rare and important. She immediately contacted a zoologist friend and colleague who confirmed the fish's identity. Scientists honored Miss Courtney-Latimer's work by naming the genus of the fish *Latimeria* after her.

Fishes with Lungs

Closely related to the lobe-finned fishes are the **lungfishes,** also called "dipnoans" (DIP-no-wons). These living fossils are a group of primitive fishes that have gills like other fish, but also have lungs similar to those of land animals. Some lungfish live in shallow, muddy waters and are often called mudfish.

The first lungfish were discovered in 1833 in the swamps of the Amazon rainforest. The South Ameri-

A coelacanth. When a living specimen of this fish was discovered in 1939 near Madagascar, scientists determined that it was closely related to fossil specimens dating back 250 million years.

(Left) An African lungfish. Lungfish belong to a group of primitive fishes that have both gills and a set of functional lungs. (Below) The paddlefish belongs to an ancient family of fish with cartilaginous skeletons.

can lungfish is about 3 feet (0.9 m) long. Since that time two other types of lungfish, one in Africa and one in Australia, have been found.

Fishes Without Bones

Another class of fishes has remained largely unchanged in form or abundance since the Devonian period in which they developed. This is the class of cartilaginous fishes. They have skeletons of tough, flexible cartilage rather than hard, rigid bones. The class includes the sharks, the rays, and the skates.

The United States boasts an example of a living fossil in the **paddlefish.** Although this primitive fish has a cartilaginous skeleton, it is only distantly related to sharks. The American paddlefish has only one close relative, a similar paddlefish that lives in Chinese lakes and waterways. The docile fish is one of America's largest freshwater species. In the thirty years of its normal life span, the fish can grow to 8 feet (2.3 m) in length and weigh more than 160 pounds (73 kg). The paddlefish has a broad, flat head and a snout like a narrow paddle that is often more than a foot long. The fish spend most of the daylight hours hiding in deep water. They feed by skimming the surface waters, filtering tiny single-celled organisms through their snouts.

Chapter Four

Survivors from the Age of Insects

A Link Between the Worms and the Insects

To find one of the oldest living fossils in the world, one need only look underfoot. **Peripatus** (pe-RIP-at-us) is a link with more than half a billion years ago. Resembling a centipede, peripatus is a bridge between segmented worms and insects. Some of its relatives became the earthworms, while others developed into the **arthropods** (meaning "jointed legs"). The arthropods include the insects, crustaceans, the arachnids (spiders), and the myriapods, the multilegged creatures the peripatus most closely resembles.

***Peripatus* forms a bridge between
segmented worms and insects.
This specimen is from Costa Rica.**

Peripatus dwells among the rotting twigs and leaves of the forest floor. Small insects, alive or dead, provide a constant food supply. Like the insects, peripatus breathes through air tubes, or spiracles. These connect the surface of its skin directly with its inner tissues. Peripatus has numerous live-born offspring. It has an unusual protective device: It can eject a gluey liquid from openings at either side of its mouth. This glop can stun and snare an attacker from as far away as a foot (0.3 m). These adaptations have helped the simple animal to survive such a long time.

Insects

Most insect groups are very ancient, but some are unrivaled in their antiquity. The **silverfish,** the **cockroach,** and the **dragonfly** were already well established in the Pennsylvanian period—some 300 million years ago. This was the age of giant insects. At that time, much of the earth was covered with shallow seas. There were great swamps, marshy deltas, and moist lowlands where insects proliferated. Primitive trees and giant horsetails produced the rich vegetation that formed the thick seams of coal under the earth. Giant dragonflies with 30-inch (76-cm) wingspans developed. Today's dragonflies are seldom more than 3 to 4 inches (7.5–10 cm) long, but otherwise they are identical.

The ancestor of all insects was probably a creeping, segmented wormlike creature similar to peripatus. It is not much of a step from this type of organism to the silverfish, one of the most primitive insects. The silverfish is wingless and shows a very simple and ancient development pattern. Most insects go through stages of development called *metamorphosis* (met-ah-MOR-foe-sis). Many species change from egg to wormlike larva to immature pupa to adult. But the silverfish develops from the egg in one step. The egg hatches into a tiny insect that is structurally identical to the adult, only smaller. The silverfish grows, but never changes in form. Most insects do not live long, but the silverfish can stay alive for several years.

Today silverfish are most commonly found as indoor pests, especially in warm, damp climates. The insects feast on the starch from book bindings, wallpaper paste, and textiles. Early silverfish apparently thrived on natural starches from vegetable matter—leaves and twigs.

Cockroaches too have a more than 300-million-year history. Sporting one of the oldest pedigrees of any living creature, cockroaches were among the first forms of insect life. They are flightless insects with rudimentary wings. During the prehistoric Carboniferous age (the age of coal) they were among the most numerous insects on earth. Some would say they still are!

Cockroaches prefer warm, damp places similar to the climate in which they first evolved and flourished. Today's cockroaches—seldom more than 1½ inches (2–3 cm) long—would be no match for the giant specimens of 300 million years ago. Scientists believe they weighed ¼ pound (114 g) or more. In a protected environment, some kinds of living roaches can come close to this size.

Other Arthropod Living Fossils

The **scorpions** are also living fossils. They are not insects but members of the order of arachnids. This is the same class of arthropods that includes spiders, mites, ticks, and the horseshoe crab. Scorpions qualify as living fossils because they have changed so little in 300 million years. However, they have shifted from a water to a land habitat.

Chapter Five

Early Land Dwellers

Amphibians and Reptiles

The amphibians were the first four-legged animals to live on land. They have existed for more than 300 million years. Modern amphibian species of frogs, toads, and salamanders evolved from earlier types.

In the past decade or two, populations and numbers of species of frogs, toads, and salamanders have begun to decline at alarming rates. This has been observed around the world. Scientists theorize that a number of factors are at work. The loss of living space through human encroachment and changes in living conditions through pollution and climate shifts may be reasons.

One group of amphibians gave rise to the **reptiles.** Some of the most spectacular survivors from the Age of Dinosaurs include living examples from the reptile family. Modern reptiles—including turtles, crocodiles, lizards, and snakes—are remnants of the once-dominant class of animals, but most are relatively modern species that are no more than a few million years old.

Some living fossils are animal types that have changed somewhat, but are still representative of ancient forms. For example, when mature, today's crocodiles are 15 to 20 feet (4.5–6 m) long. Occasionally a very old specimen may be closer to 30 feet (8 m). This makes them only about a third as long as their ancient ancestors, which grew to 50 to 60 feet (17–20 m). Only the size has changed!

The **sphenodon** (SFEE-na-don) is a lizardlike reptile that survives only on several islands off the New Zealand coast. The local Maori name for the animal is "tuatara." The reptile may be 7½ inches (19 cm) or more in length. It has remained unchanged for nearly 200 million years, since the Triassic era.

The sphenodon is the last living representative of the ancient reptilian order Rhynchocephalia (rin-ko-sef-ALE-ya), or beak-headed lizards. It has a small round hole at the base of the skull over the brain cavity. This is the site of the animal's most unusual feature:

The sphenodon, native to New Zealand,
is the only surviving representative
of an ancient order of lizards.

a small third eye that is light-sensitive but is not used for vision.

Darwin believed these third eyes to be a legacy from an earlier (and now extinct) form of life—possibly a type of fish that had a functioning third eye. A vestige of this third eye survives in the development of **mammal** embryos.

The skeleton of the sphenodon—the size of its limbs and the way the leg bones are put together—suggests a transition to a mammalian skeletal form. Biologists think that the sphenodon as well as the egg-laying mammals of Australia—the duckbill and echidna (spiny anteater)—all descended from a common amphibian ancestor.

Birds

Birds are closely related to reptiles. Birds are characterized by feathers that are thought to be modified scales. Some scientists regard birds as today's living dinosaurs. The most primitive kinds of living birds are flightless ones, including kiwis, ostriches, and penguins. Among the birds that fly, albatrosses have a very long history.

Penguins have been around for about 50 million years. We know this because fossil remains very similar

(Above) The Galápagos penguin lives on the Galápagos Islands off the coast of Ecuador. Penguins are among the most primitive types of birds. (Right) The notornis is an endangered, flightless bird. It was believed to be extinct prior to its rediscovery in New Zealand.

to today's penguins have been found in Antarctica. Today's penguins are considerably smaller than earlier types. Twenty-five million years ago, penguins stood 5 feet (1.5 m) tall and weighed between 200 and 300 pounds (90–180 kg), whereas today's penguins are about half that size.

The **notornis** (no-TOR-nis) is a bird about the size of a chicken with beautiful blue and green plumage. It was long believed extinct until examples of the rare species turned up in New Zealand. Deer and stoats (a weasel-like animal), both introduced to New Zealand by man, are the two greatest threats to the notornis's survival. Deer often trample the birds' nests. And stoats like to eat the eggs, chicks, and young birds.

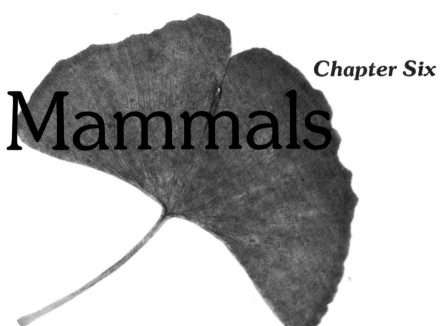

Chapter Six

Mammals

Mammals are the most highly evolved animals. They are also the youngest class of vertebrates. Mammals first appeared in the Jurassic age, but have become more numerous and widely diversified only in the past 65 million years. Therefore it may seem surprising that some types of mammals have a very long history and can qualify as living fossils.

There are three broad categories of mammals: **placentals, marsupials,** and **monotremes**.

The Placental Mammals

The placental mammals include humans. The offspring develop inside the mother by means of the placenta—a special organ that exchanges fluids and gases between the mother and the growing fetus.

Rodents, including mice, rats, and squirrels, are the most diversified order of placental mammals. They are distinguished by teeth that continue to grow throughout the individual's life span. Among rodents, we find a living fossil in the squirrel, which has changed very little in about 35 million years.

The Monotremes

Monotremes are the most primitive type of mammal. They share several characteristics with the reptiles they developed from. Monotremes lay eggs and have a single body opening, or cloaca, that is used both for elimination and reproduction.

There are three known examples of monotremes —Australia's platypus and spiny anteater (echidna), and a species of anteater similar to the echidna that lives in New Guinea. The monotremes probably date back to the Triassic era (some 200 million years ago). They are warm-blooded, but their body temperatures are several degrees cooler than those of other mammals. Female monotremes nurse their young by lying on their backs. The young do not suck the milk but simply lap it up with their tongues. They are distin-

The monotremes are egg-laying mammals. Two examples are the duckbill platypus (above) and the spiny anteater, which is also known as the echidna (right).

guished by small lower jaws. Teeth are not present in the adult, but in the early stages of monotreme development the animals have large teeth.

The Marsupials

Marsupials give birth to incompletely developed offspring that continue their development in an exterior pouch (marsupium) on the mother's body.

The New World boasts what is probably the earliest surviving marsupial. The **opossum** dates back at least 120 million years. It developed in the late Mesozoic era and is widely distributed. Through the intervening ages, the opossum has undergone few changes. Opossums have small brains, five-toed feet, and **prehensile** tails. They are also very prolific.

The opossum is probably the oldest surviving mammal that is not a monotreme. Opossums share a very primitive feature with the marsupials found in other parts of the world—a pouch for carrying the young babies.

Opossums are shy and retiring. They are nocturnal and are seldom seen, even though they are very common. Their sharp teeth make them able to eat a widely varied diet. Because of their ability to "play dead," they have frequently been able to escape death from

The Tasmanian devil is a marsupial predator native
to the island of Tasmania, south of Australia.

larger and smarter predators. They have also outlived many species of more intelligent animals.

Australia is home to some 200 types of unique mammals. Except for the two monotreme species, most of the rest are marsupials. They are also all living fossils. They range from the giant **kangaroo** to the tiny, golden-furred **marsupial mole**. There are **marsupial cats, flying squirrels, koalas**, and **wombats**.

The island of Tasmania, south of Australia, offers two further examples of marsupial predators—the extinct striped **Tasmanian tiger** and the **Tasmanian devil.**

Australia's geographic **isolation** led to the survival of so many primitive mammal forms there. The continent is a zoological garden of living fossils.

Chapter Seven

The Plant Kingdom

The plant kingdom is rich in examples of living fossils. As life evolved from the simple to the more complex, it left behind many examples of the types of plants that developed along the way.

The lower plant forms such as algaes, club mosses, and horsetails may all be regarded as living fossils. But among the more advanced seed-bearing and flowering plants that predominate today, some organisms maintain more ancient features than most of their modern relatives. Most of our trees and garden flowers have evolved in the past few million years.

Giant plant forms—treelike ferns, horsetails, and

lycopods (lie-ka-pods)—predominated during the Carboniferous age and predated all of our modern trees. The giant lycopods or club mosses died out in the early Permian age. Today the stubby **creeping club moss**, the *lycopodium* (like-o-PODE-ee-yum), is one of the only living representatives. The giant horsetails that developed during the Carboniferous age had largely died off by the early Permian. Today only some species of small horsetails survive, although they differ only slightly from their giant ancestors.

The ginkgo tree is of special interest. The species is a survivor of a once huge division of the plant group known as the *gymnosperms* that was widespread in the Mesozoic era. During the transition period from spore-bearing to seed-bearing plants, the naked-seed plants, the gymnosperms, developed. In gymnosperms the immature seed is not protected by tissue but is exposed.

The ginkgo is a tall, woody tree that reaches a height of about 100 feet (30 m). It branches outward repeatedly to form a spreading crown. Ginkgo leaves are identical to fossil specimens that date back as far as the Triassic Age—over 200 million years ago.

The ginkgo grows naturally only in China and Japan. But because it is hardy, the tree has become a popular exotic plant cultivated in gardens around the world. Ginkgos are very resistant to fire, cold weather, insect pests, and funguses. They grow well in cities. The

(Left) Modern horsetails are smaller in size than their prehistoric ancestors, but remarkably similar in other characteristics. (Right) The ancestors of the modern tree fern date back to the Mesozoic era.

ginkgo was introduced into Europe from Japan around 1690 by Engelbrecht Kaempfer, a Dutch physician.

Gingoales, a class of plants related to the ginkgo, were once widespread on the earth. The first ginkgo fossils were found in Italy. Since then, fossil remains of the graceful tree have been found on every continent except Africa. Botanists believe, however, that fossils of African ginkgos will one day be found.

Conifers (or cone-bearing plants) are another class of gymnosperm. When the angiosperms (or flowering plants) began proliferating during the Cretaceous age (some 135 million years ago), the conifers declined somewhat in diversity. But they remain a varied and flourishing group throughout temperate and upland portions of the world. The types of living conifers range in size from the giant sequoia to the dwarf juniper.

(Above) A King Sago palm in Florida, a cycad. At one time 40 percent of all the plants in the world were cycads. Today, only four types survive in the United States. (Below) The *Welwitschia mirabilis* is an ancient dwarf tree found in the Namibian Desert of Africa.

Some species of conifer can live for 3,000 years or more (for example, the bristlecone pine), making them the earth's oldest living things.

A true rarity of the plant kingdom is *Welwitschia mirabilis* (well-witcha meer-A-bill-iss), found only in Africa's Namibian Desert. This is a type of dwarf tree with a trunk never more than 2 feet (0.6 m) off the ground. Yet it may have a diameter of about 4 feet (1.2 m) and a circumference of as much as 14 feet (3.2 m). The tree is anchored to the ground by a huge taproot about 5 feet (1.5 m) long. The long leaves of the plant are about 4 feet (1.2 m) wide, but split apart easily in the wind because of their parallel veins. The Welwitschia dates from about 250 million years ago.

People have had a hand in repopulating the earth with some plant species that might have been close to extinction. In general, efforts to rescue plant species have been more successful than attempts to keep animal species alive.

Chapter Eight

Living Fossils: Today and Tomorrow

Are There Monsters Out There?

Many of our living fossils were found years after scientists became convinced that these life-forms were already extinct. Persistent tales of creatures such as the Loch Ness monster, the American "Bigfoot" (Sasquatch) of the Pacific Northwest, or the Abominable Snowman of the Himalayas could contain some kernel of truth. Perhaps some unknown survivors or "missing links" from vanished species still exist in these places.

Some scientists think it is possible—though unlikely—that a few medium-sized dinosaurs could still exist in remote portions of Africa or South America. There are occasional reports of sightings of such a beast or of a flying reptile. But no one has yet produced any hard evidence. Most likely the observers just did not know what they were looking at.

Stories of monsters do underscore one quality that many true living fossils seem to have: the ability to keep themselves hidden, thus avoiding threats from human or other predators.

New Life from Old

Although such speculation is still in the realm of science fiction, scientists may one day be able to actually reconstruct plants and animals of the past. They would do this through genetic engineering and DNA reconstruction. DNA (which stands for deoxyribonucleic acid) provides the blueprint for all life forms. It is the arrangement of the components of DNA that determines how genes are able to create and transmit the characteristics that make up any organism.

Scientists today are beginning to "read" the messages that are encoded in the DNA molecules of living plants and animals. If they can someday interpret particles of DNA from long-dead or extinct organisms, they may actually be able to reconstruct such plants or animals! Preserved animal tissues—fragments of bone or animal tissues preserved in ice, peat, or by other means—might yield samples of DNA.

Tomorrow's Fossils

In the tree of life, some life-forms die off. Others continue, making few or no changes. Others flourish. Or they may change and evolve into new successful types. There are no clear-cut reasons why certain plants and animals have become living fossils. One of the reasons may be adaptability. Another may be luck.

In order to survive, a plant or animal species must gradually adapt to changing conditions. These adaptations allow the organisms to capture food, move from place to place, protect themselves, and rear their young more successfully than their competitors.

The mechanisms that led to certain species' becoming living fossils in the past are still at work today. Some species are dying off and others are surviving, perhaps only by the skin of their teeth, and perhaps not for long.

Today's living species of plants and animals could become tomorrow's living fossils.

Adaptation. A change in an organism's characteristics that enables it to survive better in a certain environment.

Amphibian. A type of vertebrate that has gills in the immature stage but can breathe air in the adult stage. Amphibians are cold-blooded and without scales.

Anatomy. The internal structure and organization of an organism.

Arthropod. An invertebrate animal with jointed legs and a segmented body.

Breeding population. Plants or animals of a single species that interbreed within their own group because of geographic isolation.

Differentiation. The development of new animal types or species from existing ones.

Distribution. The range of geographical areas where a certain type of organism lives.

Evolution. The gradual change of life-forms over the period of many generations.

Fossils. The evidence or remains of previously existing life-forms.

Gene pool. The total genetic material (including the

range of possible traits) available within a breeding population.

Genetics. The branch of biology that deals with the transmittal and inheritance of characteristics from one generation to another.

Genus. In taxonomy, the next higher level (above species) of classification of organisms.

Insect. A member of a class of arthropods with six legs and three main body segments.

Isolation. The long-term separation of a group of organisms from others with whom they might breed.

Longevity. The life span of an individual organism or the length of time a type or group of organisms survives.

Mammal. A warm-blooded, usually hairy vertebrate that feeds milk to its offspring. All mammals have hair at some point in their lives.

Marsupial. A type of mammal that nurses its incompletely developed offspring in a pouch (called a marsupium).

Monotreme. The most primitive type of mammal, a monotreme lays eggs and has a single organ, called a cloaca, for reproduction and elimination.

Mutation. A change in individual genes or in their arrangement that leads to a change in characteristics that can be inherited by offspring.

Natural selection. A theory of evolution in which

nature "selects" the fittest, or best-adapted, individuals for survival and reproduction.

Organism. A living being.

Paleobiology. The study of ancient life-forms.

Paleontologist. A scientist who studies the fossil records of ancient life-forms.

Placentals. Mammals whose offspring develop inside the mother by means of a placenta.

Population. A group of individuals of the same species in a geographic area.

Prehensile tail. A tail adapted for seizing or grasping by wrapping around.

Reptile. A member of the class of cold-blooded vertebrates with lungs, a bony skeleton, and (unlike the amphibians) scales or horned plates.

Species. A unit of classification in taxonomy. All members of a species are potentially able to interbreed.

Taxonomy. The scientific system for classifying plants and animals.

Trait. A specific characteristic of a plant or animal that may be inherited.

Variation. The range of differences found among individual members of a species.

For Further Reading

Arnold, Caroline. *Trapped in Tar: Fossils from the Ice Age.* New York: Clarion Books, 1987.

Fisher, David E. *The Origin and Evolution of Our Own Particular Universe.* New York: Atheneum, 1988.

Gallant, Roy A. *Before the Sun Dies: The Story of Evolution.* New York: Macmillan, 1989.

Lauber, Patricia. *Dinosaurs Walked Here and Other Stories Fossils Tell.* New York: Bradbury Press, 1987.

Miller, Susanne S. *Prehistoric Mammals.* New York: Messner, 1984.

Skelton, Renee. *Charles Darwin.* New York: Barron's, 1987.

Smith, Howard E. *Living Fossils.* New York: Dodd, Mead, 1982.

Stidworthy, John. *Mighty Mammals of the Past.* Englewood Cliffs, NJ.: Silver, 1987.

Thomson, Keith Stewart. *Living Fossil: The Story of the Coelacanth.* New York: W. W. Norton, 1991.

There are also several older, out-of-print books on the subject that you may be able to locate on your library shelves.